The Burr-Hamilton
Duel
and Related Matters

Other Publications Concerning the Life and Career of Colonel Aaron Burr by this Author

Colonel Aaron Burr: The American Phoenix, New York, Exposition Press, Inc., 1961. Revised and enlarged edition, 1964. Cloth binding, 114 pages.

Colonel Aaron Burr: The Misunderstood Man, San Antonio, Texas, The Naylor Company, 1967. Cloth binding, 155 pages, 10 Pen & Ink Illustrations.

Napoleon's Dossier On Aaron Burr, San Antonio, Texas, The Naylor Company, 1969. Soft cover. 76 pages.

"In defense of Aaron Burr," *The Virginia Magazine of History,* October, 1952. Vol. 60, No. 4, pp. 582-590.

"Another Shot in the Burr-Hamilton Duel," *Manuscripts,* (The Manuscript Society), Summer Issue, 1957. Vol. IX, No. 3, pp. 192-194.

"The Aaron Burr Bicentennial," *Manuscripts,* (The Manuscript Society), Winter Issue, 1957. Vol. IX, No. 1, pp. 26-27.

"A. Burr: Historians' Foil," The *Lodestar* of the American University, Washington, D. C., Summer Issue, 1965. Vol. 10, No. 2, pp. 5-10. Illustrated.

"Aaron Burr of New York," The *Yorker,* (New York State Historical Association), March-April, 1958. Vol. XVI, No. 4, pp. 10-13.

"Mrs. Aaron Burr's Passport of 1853," *Autograph Collectors' Journal,* Summer Issue, 1951. Vol. III, No. 4, pp. 13-17. One illustration.

"To Give Honor Where Honor Is Long Overdue," An address concerning the Reverend Aaron Burr and Colonel Aaron Burr, delivered May 17, 1950, published in: *Historic Newark in Bronze,* John T. McSharry, Editor; published by The Schoolmen's Club of Newark, New Jersey, 1966 (revised edition). pp. 64-70.

"Colonel Aaron Burr in Ohio," *Sterling Sparks,* Sterling Grinding Wheel Co., Tiffin, Ohio, August, 1949. Vol. 8, No. 6, pp. 4-5. One illustration.

The Burr-Hamilton
Duel
and Related Matters

by SAMUEL ENGLE BURR, JR., Ed.D.

The Naylor Company
Book Publishers of the Southwest
San Antonio, Texas

FIRST EDITION, January, 1971

2nd Printing, February, 1971

SECOND EDITION, December, 1971

Preface

FOR 200 YEARS, there have been certain writers who have played the part of character assassins, industriously working against the cause of Col. Aaron Burr. They seem to have derived an unholy kind of sadistic joy and perverted satisfaction from exaggerating his errors or weaknesses and from minimizing his good qualities and his strengths. Not only that — they have fabricated rather improbable or even quite impossible faults and have ascribed them to him. They have poured upon him unbridled vituperation for the assumed lack of this or that virtue or for having transgressed against this or that standard of behavior. They have ranted and railed about some facts which have been on the dark side while they have blithely trampled into the absorbing dust of time some facts which would make Colonel Burr appear to be a patriot and a hero.[1]

---

1 Several years ago, the author of this present book had an interview with a well-known historian who had written rather unfavorably about Colonel Burr's part in the election of 1800 and about the Burr Expedition to the West. This historian was asked: "In the course of your research about these matters, how many original Burr documents did you consult?" The question obviously surprised and embarrassed him. After a bit of hesitation, he replied: "I must admit that I never have seen an original Burr document. Everything that I have written about Colonel Burr has been based on secondary sources and possibly upon quite biased secondary sources at that."

"But why? Why didn't you go to the few original materials that are available? Why didn't you do some original research?"

"Well, I suppose that I considered that the place of Aaron Burr in America history had been pretty well settled by those who had written before I did. I just accepted their judgment and repeated what they had written."

The result of this has been that the American public has been misinformed, misled and ill-advised concerning the life and career of Col. Aaron Burr. He fully deserves to be looked upon as one of the great men who served this nation well, during the American Revolution, during the early Nationalist Period of U.S. history and even after he no longer was openly active in the military and political fields. But ways and means have been found to make him appear to have been a demon or a villain and to have been a less desirable and less honorable character than he really was. The public has been shown a very distorted image of him. He not only was the contemporary of great men (Washington, Adams, Ward, Hamilton, Jay, Marshall, the Pinckneys, Mason, Jefferson, Gallatin, Clinton, Madison, Monroe, etc.); in many ways, he was their equal.[2]

Perhaps it will be helpful to consider a specific example (at least twenty-five or thirty others could be chosen) of a way in which the propaganda machine has been used in order to downgrade Col. Aaron Burr. The example chosen for consideration here is as follows:

The American Past, an illustrated history of the United States, by Roger Butterfield, was published in 1947.[3]

This rather elaborate book, with 1,000 illustrations, includes reproductions of many portraits. Portraits of many of the Founding Fathers are in the volume: Franklin, Washington, Adams, Jefferson, Hamilton, Madison, Monroe, and others. Burr is presented in the volume twice — but not by a portrait, although portraits by Gilbert Stuart, John Vanderlyn, Henry Inman, James Vandyck and others were available. Burr is presented by a copy of a crayon drawing (page

[2] Schachner, Nathan; *Aaron Burr; A Biography*, New York, A. S. Barnes and Co., Inc., Perpetua Edition (Paperback), 1961, Page 516. "In an age of giants, he, too, was of the elect."

[3] Butterfield, Roger; *The American Past*, New York, Simon & Schuster, Inc., 1947. (See pp. 33 and 45)

33) and by another drawing which amounts to a caricature (page 45). In connection with the second drawing, the author (Butterfield) reported that at the age of eighty years, Burr was "toothless, spindle-shanked and forgotten."

The intent of this statement surely must have been to convey an anti-Burr impression — to create an anti-Burr milieu or atmosphere.

Nowhere in Butterfield's rather large volume (476 quarto pages) is there a similar reference as to the number of natural teeth which any other prominent man still had when he reached the age of eighty years. Nor is there any reference to the "shanks" of any other great political leader.

Butterfield might have directed the attention of his readers to the fact than many of Burr's associates in the field of politics did not live to celebrate their eightieth birthdays. John Adams and Thomas Jefferson were exceptions to this, but Washington died at the age of sixty-seven years, George Clinton at the age of seventy-three years, Philip Schuyler at the age of seventy-one years, Rufus King at the age of seventy-two years, etc.

Butterfield might have called attention to the fact that Burr was the head of a group of successful lawyers after his return from Europe in 1812 and that he was active in the group, practically to the day of his death in 1836.

He might have recorded that Burr had remarried when he was seventy-seven years old. His second wife was Mme. Eliza Bowen Jumel, who was twenty-two years younger than he was. Their honeymoon was a trip to Hartford, Connecticut where they were honored guests in the governor's mansion. The governor at that time happened to be Colonel Burr's cousin, Henry W. Edwards.

Butterfield might have said that even in his old age, Colonel Burr did have a considerable number of attentive friends and some interested relatives although it must be recognized that one of the penalties which a man pays for the privilege of living to the age of eighty years is this: He must see most of his friends die before he does. A man who dies while in the "prime of life" may be mourned by many friends who survive him but an octogenarian has witnessed the death and burial of most of his friends. It should be realized that Colonel Burr achieved a life of four-score years, even though it included several periods of unusual physical hardship.[4] But Butterfield did not report such things. What he did was to report that Burr was "tooth-less, spindle-shanked and forgotten."[5]

The question may well be asked: "Just how much vim, vigor, vitality and virility did Butterfield expect Burr to have, at the age of eighty years?" Isn't it rather remarkable that Colonel Burr even lived to attain that age? Isn't it worthy of note that he remained active and alert practically until the time of his death?

As has been the case in other matters concerned with the life and career of Col. Aaron Burr, this adverse reference by Butterfield was not allowed to remain only in *The American Past*. Someone else, apparently with the anti-Burr position to record, seized upon this abuse of Burr and repeated it. This was done in 1968, in a Focus Book, *The Burr-Hamilton Duel*, by Ralph Knight.[6]

---

[4] Colonel Burr lived before the era of vitamin and aspirin pills, anti-biotics, wonder drugs, flouride toothpaste, blood transfusions, hormone treatments, X-ray pictures, oxygen masks, face lifting, heart and kidney transplants, enriched bread, homogenized milk, frozen orange juice, iodized salt, etc. etc.

Even with these aids to health now available to them what do present-day authors expect for themselves when (and if) they reach the age of eighty years? Will they still have all of their natural teeth? Will they still have shapely legs and well-turned ankles? And will they receive daily visits from throngs of admiring friends?

[5] George Washington died on December 14, 1799. For some time before his death, he had a full set of false teeth. But historians do not refer to Washington as having been "toothless." (See *Time*, The Weekly Newsmagazine, Nov. 8, 1971, Vol. 98, No. 19, Page 52.)

[6] Knight, Ralph; *The Burr-Hamilton Duel*, New York, Franklin Watts, Inc., 1968.

In this book, on page fifty-eight, there is the same drawing (a caricature) of Burr[7] which appeared on page forty-five of the Butterfield volume, with the caption: "Toothless and forgotten, former Vice-President Aaron Burr lingered on until he was 80 years old." And on page fifty-seven of his book, Knight reported that Burr was "toothless and spindly." All of which has the sound of derision and vindictiveness.[8]

Another method which has been used from time to time in the process of abusing and defaming Colonel Burr has been the use of the propaganda device known as "The Big Lie." This device is that the bigger the lie that is told, the greater the likelihood that it will be believed.

For example, in *Parade*, The Sunday Newspaper Magazine, there is a regular feature called: "Walter Scott's Personality Parade." In the issue of the magazine dated October 17, 1971 part of one of the questions presented in this feature asked which vice-president of the United States had been charged with "high crimes and misdemeanors in office." The editor's answer which was published was: "Vice-President Aaron Burr."[9]

Insofar as the recorded facts of history are concerned, this answer constituted a "Big Lie." It was absolutely false.

The career of Col. Aaron Burr as vice-president of the United States was most honorable. His record in that office was impeccable. Even his enemies, who were trying to

---

[7] This same caricature of Burr was used as an illustration (page 143) in the book *The Great Conspiracy*, by Donald Barr Chidsey, published by Crown Publishers, Inc., New York, 1967. The caption was: "The Last Days of Aaron Burr," with no reference to his lack of teeth or to his "spindle shanks," or to his assumed lack of "friends." There usually is some malicious intent in the drawing of caricatures.

[8] Colonel Burr's dentist, during the 1830s, was Dr. Dodge of New York City. There is a record showing that he paid a goodly sum for a set of dentures, in 1834, two years before his death. (Stillwell, John E., *The Burr Portraits*, privately printed, 1928, p. 103.)

[9] *Parade*, The Sunday Newspaper Magazine, New York, Parade Publications, Inc., October 17, 1971, Page 2.

destroy him politically, never had anything adverse to say about his service as vice-president. It is a matter of authenticated fact that his enemies joined with his friends in praising the manner in which he handled the vice-presidential position.

At the end of his four year term as vice-president (it ended on March 4, 1805), the United States Senate passed a resolution to the effect "that the thanks of the Senate be presented to Aaron Burr, as testimony of the impartiality and ability with which he has presided over their deliberations, and of their entire approbation of his conduct in the discharge of the arduous and important duties assigned to him as president of the Senate." This resolution was passed by a unanimous vote, with both the Republicans and Federalists voting for it.

Charges against Colonel Burr were presented at two periods in the course of his life. In neither case did the charges have anything to do with his conduct as a public official.

After the Burr-Hamilton duel, Colonel Burr was charged with a misdemeanor in New York and with murder in New Jersey. Neither charge ever was pressed and no warrant was served as a result of them. Also, at the time of the Burr Expedition to the West, charges were made against Colonel Burr. He was accused of treason and misprision of treason (concealing knowledge of treason). Trials on these charges were held in the state of Kentucky, the territory of Mississippi and at Richmond, Virginia. In each case, Colonel Burr was found "not guilty."

What a travesty all of this is, upon the business of recording serious history! And, any study of the life and career of Col. Aaron Burr should be regarded as a matter of serious history.

To the author of this present book on the Burr-Hamilton duel, it always has seemed that the duel was not the most important event in the life and career of Col. Aaron Burr. It should not be permitted to overshadow many other important things that deserve to be kept in the record. For example, such important matters as these:

Choosing law rather than religion as a life work.
His marriage to Mrs. Theodosia Bartow Prevost of "The Hermitage."[10]
Three terms of office in the New York State Legislature.
Drafting the charter for The Manhattan Company.
Using the Tammany Society as the basis for an effective political "machine."
The idea of multiple ownership of land as a means to break the property qualification for voters.
Opposition to the institution of slavery in New York State.
The concept that women can become educated.
The marriage of his daughter, Theodosia, to Joseph Alston of South Carolina.
Service as the attorney general for the state of New York.
Service as a United States senator for six years.
Carrying New York State for the Democratic-Republicans in the national election of 1800.
Service as vice-president of the United States for four years.
Serving as chairman of the New York State Constitutional Convention.
Favoring the purchase of Louisiana from France.
Conducting a fair trial for Assoc. Justice Samuel Chase.

10 See: "Mrs. Prevost Requests the Honor of His Company. . . ." by Dorothy V. Smith, Manuscripts, Vol. XI, No. 4, (Fall, 1950).

Recognition of John Vanderlyn's artistic talent.
Conducting a successful defense when falsely charged with treason.
Guest of honor at the coronation of King Charles XIII of Sweden.
Proposing a practical plan for the liberation of Mexico.
Handling the Mecdef Eden case in a masterful way.
Calling attention to the appeal of the West.

Because matters such as these have seemed to be more important, the duel has received scant attention in this writer's previous books on Col. Aaron Burr. It seems, however, that other writers repeatedly over-emphasize the duel and its importance. They persist in bringing the duel to public attention.

As a result, this book has been written. It was published in January, 1971 and a second printing was published in February, 1971. Only about a dozen copies of these two printings remain and they will be kept "for the record."

The present "Revised Edition" contains this new preface and about thirty-seven new paragraphs in the text. Several errors — chiefly in spelling — which were in the first two printings, have been corrected.

Samuel Engle Burr, Jr.

Fort Worth, Texas
   and
Linden, Virginia

Contents

Part I: A Background of Continual Rivalry

A ARON BURR (the younger) was born at Newark, New
Jersey, February 6, 1756. Soon afterward, the Burr fam-
ily moved to Princeton. It was there that Rev. Aaron
Burr died, on September 24, 1757. His wife, Esther Edwards
Burr, died on April 7, 1758. Following these tragic events,
Aaron and his sister Sarah, who always was called Sally,
were taken to the home of Dr. Shippen,[1] in Philadelphia.

Soon, they became the wards of their maternal uncle,
Rev. Timothy Edwards, who had established his home at
Elizabethtown, New Jersey (now known as Elizabeth).

---

[1] There was a close personal friendship between the Burr family of
Newark and Princeton and the Shippen family of Philadelphia. Dr.
Edward Shippen had been one of the "founding fathers" of the College
of New Jersey. Dr. William Shippen, Sr., went to Princeton to help fight
the epidemic of smallpox, in 1757-1758. Dr. William Shippen, Jr., graduated
from the College of New Jersey in 1754 as the valedictorian of his class.
Later, he was associated with his father, in the practice of medicine, in
Philadelphia.

Uncle Timothy, assisted by several tutors (one of whom was Tapping Reeve[2]), provided Aaron's educational program until he was ready to enter college.

Alexander Hamilton was born on the small island of Nevis, in the British West Indies. There has been controversy as to the date of his birth. It may have been January 11, 1757 but the event may have taken place in 1756, or even a year earlier. He remained in the West Indies until 1772, when he took ship for Boston — arriving there near the end of October. From Boston, he traveled by stagecoach to New York, where he presented letters of introduction to several persons of importance in the community. They sent him to the school maintained by Master Francis Barber at Elizabethtown, New Jersey. There, he prepared to enter college.

It is quite possible that these two young men saw one another — passed one another on the street — may even have said "Good morning" to one another, occasionally, in Elizabethtown, in 1773, but there is no record to indicate that they came to know one another then. At any rate, there was no rivalry between them at that time. And, they attended different colleges: Burr graduated from the College of New Jersey (now Princeton University) and Hamilton graduated from King's College (now Columbia University).

Aaron Burr and Alexander Hamilton began their rivalry when both of them were young officers on the staff of Gen. George Washington early in the American Revolution. At this stage of their relationship, they saw one another frequently, during a period of a few months, while the commander-in-chief of the Patriot forces maintained his

---

2 Tapping Reeve married Sally Burr, Aaron's sister. After their marriage, they lived at Litchfield, Connecticut, where he established a law school.

headquarters in the Roger Morris mansion at the upper end of Manhattan Island, New York. No doubt they came into some contact with one another at other places in and near New York City.

As a volunteer in the Patriot cause, Burr preferred to be with troops in the field; at his own request, he was transferred to Gen. Israel Putnam's command. Apparently, Hamilton preferred desk work, at the very center of things, and he continued to serve as an aide to General Washington for the major portion of his time in the Revolutionary army. Toward the end of the war, he did have experience in the field, at the Battle of Yorktown (October, 1781). After that engagement he was placed on the inactive list of officers.

As soon as possible, after their active duty as officers in the Patriot forces had ended, both Burr and Hamilton became lawyers. For a short time, Burr's law office was in Albany but he soon moved with his family to New York City, where Hamilton already had his law office. Again they were rivals and frequently they appeared in court, on opposite sides of this or that case. There were some occasions, however, when they appeared together as co-counsel in some legal action. It was not long before they were looked upon as the two leading lawyers of their era in New York City and New York State.

The family backgrounds of the two men may have contributed to their rivalry — especially the background from which Hamilton came.

Burr had distinguished ancestors who had been prominent in politics, government and religion during the British colonial period in America. He had been born into a social status where leadership was the natural and expected thing. On the other hand, Hamilton's original status was that of an illegitimate son, born on an obscure island, out of the mainstream of colonial expansion. He came to New York from the West Indies without social or family backing, when he was about fifteen or sixteen years of age. By his own efforts and because of his own abilities, he was able to make a place for himself. And by his marriage to Elizabeth, the daughter of Gen. Philip Schuyler, he attained full social acceptance — even social superiority.[3]

Of course, it should be noted that no one is responsible for the circumstances of his own birth. The parents were responsible for Hamilton's illegitimacy. But the ugly fact was in Hamilton's mind and it must have influenced some of his thoughts and his acts.

The Burrs and the Hamiltons very definitely accepted one another as social equals, in the early nationalist period of our history, after the American Revolution. Each of the men regarded the other as a "gentleman." They were guests in one another's homes. Theodosia Burr (Aaron's daughter) and Angelica Hamilton (Alexander's daughter) associated together on a friendly basis. Aaron Burr and Alexander Hamilton were members of the same organizations, supported the same "worthy causes" and had the same circle of friends.

But it seems that under the surface, each one may have felt some degree of uncertainty about this apparent social equality. In it, there was involved a more-or-less latent element of rivalry. Especially in Hamilton's thinking, there was the constant understanding that he had made his own way — that he had built his own reputation. Not that Burr ever boasted about his family connections — in fact, he seemed to pay little attention to his ancestry.

---

3 Colonel Burr had married Mrs. Theodosia Bartow Prevost, the daughter of Theodosius Bartow, a prominent merchant of New York City. She was the widow of Lt. Col. Jacques Marcus Prevost of the British army and the cousin-in-law of Gen. (Sir) George Prevost, governor of New Brunswick and Nova Scotia, and (later) of upper and lower Canada.

4

It is generally recognized that the greatest rivalry between Burr and Hamilton developed in the political arena. To the surprise of many, it was Burr who was the liberal, the Republican, the Democrat and it was Hamilton who was the conservative, the Federalist, the establishment!

As a follower, a devotee, a disciple of Washington, Hamilton was ready to suggest a monarchy in America. He believed that there should be a small, select privileged class. He referred to the common people as "that great beast." As a consequence, he was appointed to serve in Washington's cabinet, as the first secretary of the treasury.

On the other hand, Burr did not hesitate to criticize Washington and to differ with some of his policies. He became an anti-Federalist and an avowed Democrat or Republican. (These two terms were used almost interchangeably from 1795 to 1805. Sometimes they were put together: Democratic-Republican.)

Hamilton inclined toward the British system of government while Burr was fascinated by the French political philosophy of liberty, fraternity and equality.

Both Burr and Hamilton held a number of political positions in the early days of the American Republic. Burr was elected to his positions, except that of attorney general of the state of New York, while Hamilton was appointed to the positions which he held. Hamilton never exposed himself as a candidate who might be defeated by "the people." Burr was quite willing to "run" as a candidate and to abide by the results of the election.

Colonel Burr was elected to serve three terms in the New York State Legislature. Gov. George Clinton appointed him in 1789 to serve as attorney general for the state. This appointment automatically made him a land commissioner for the state, also. In January 1791, he was elected to membership in the United States Senate (the opposing

5

candidate was Gen. Philip Schuyler, father-in-law of General Hamilton). His six-year term in the U.S. Senate ran from 1791 to 1797.

In the national presidential election of 1792, Colonel Burr received one electoral vote, from South Carolina. In the national presidential election of 1796, Colonel Burr received thirty electoral votes.[4]

In the national presidential election of 1800, both Thomas Jefferson and Aaron Burr received seventy-three electoral votes. In accordance with the provisions of the U.S. Constitution, the election then went to the "old" House of Representatives which chose Jefferson to be president. Burr automatically became vice-president, (1801-1805). While serving as vice-president, Burr was chosen to be a member of the commission to revise the New York State Constitution and he was chosen to be the chairman of this body. In 1804, he ran as an independent Republican candidate for governor of New York and was defeated by Judge Morgan Lewis, the regular Republican candidate.

Hamilton's political career followed quite a different pattern. In 1782 he was appointed by Robert Morris to be receiver of continental taxes for New York. In 1782 and 1783, Hamilton was a member of the Continental Congress, appointed by the governor. He was a delegate to the Annapolis Convention (1786) — appointed by the New York State

---

[4] In the national election of 1796, electoral votes were thrown around rather indiscriminately. As a result, thirteen men received electoral votes. But even though Hamilton then was at the height of his political power, no elector thought it fitting or proper to cast a vote for him, for the presidency.

In this national election, there were 276 electoral votes (138 electors, each having two votes). The wide distribution of votes, among so many candidates, appears to have resulted from the desire, on the part of some electors, to honor "favorite sons," in certain states. All of the New York State votes, however, were cast for John Adams of Massachusetts and Thomas Pinckney of South Carolina. There was no honoring of Hamilton as a "favorite son."

Legislature. And in 1787, he was a member of the state legislature. He was chosen to be a representative of the state of New York in the body which came to be the Constitutional Convention (1787). In 1788, he was a member of the New York State Convention which, after much delay, ratified the U.S. Constitution for that state. Under the new national government, Hamilton served in the first presidential cabinet appointed by Washington, as secretary of the treasury, from April 1789 till January 1795. Very briefly — for a few weeks — during the Whiskey Rebellion in Pennsylvania (1794), he also was acting secretary of war. He never received any electoral votes for the presidency and he held no political position after 1795. However, Burr and Hamilton continued to be political rivals after 1795: Burr as an active Democratic-Republican and Hamilton as a behind-the-scenes Federalist.

Banking facilities are essential for any society which is engaged in trade, business and commerce. In the infant republic of the United States, business matters constantly were increasing in importance but financial facilities were not well developed. To meet the very apparent need, Hamilton proposed the establishment of the Bank of the United States. Legislation providing for such an institution was adopted by the Congress and approved by the president. The bank was established in 1791 and continued to operate until 1811. Its main office was in Philadelphia. There were branch offices in eight other cities, including New York City.

In New York City there also was a successful private bank — the Bank of New York. It was controlled by prominent Federalists who made it difficult or even impossible for anti-Federalists (Republicans) to secure credit or to negotiate loans for their commercial enterprises.

It was Col. Aaron Burr who devised a means for break-

7

ing the strangle hold of the Federalist financiers. Hamilton, of course, was included in the Federalist group.

In his capacity as a member of the New York State Assembly, Burr introduced a bill in 1799 entitled: "An Act for Supplying the City of New York with Pure and Wholesome Water." The capitalization was set at $2,000,000. Its final provision — beyond the establishment of the water company — was that: "It shall and may be lawful for the said company to employ all such surplus capital as may belong or accrue to the said company in the purchase of public or other stock, or in any other monied transactions or operations not inconsistent with the Constitution and laws of this state or of the United States, for the sole benefit of said company."

As a result of this act, and especially as a result of its final clause, the Bank of the Manhattan Company came into being on September 1, 1799.[5]

The Federalists — especially those who had controlled the banking business and most especially Hamilton — were furious. They had lost their control over money matters in New York and they held Burr accountable for this development.

Landed and moneyed citizens of the state of New York had the right to vote, after the adoption of the Constitution and the formation of the federal union. But the less wealthy people, the poor people, the common men were not granted the franchise. For example, it was necessary to own a "free-hold" worth at least £100 in order to vote for a state senator. And the men with money were quite likely to be Federalists.

Again, it was Burr who saw a method by which this restrictive system could be broken.

---

[5] The Bank of the Manhattan Company continues to exist, with various changes, as "The Chase Manhattan Bank." The water company continued to supply "pure and wholesome water" until 1835.

Colonel Burr asked three relatively poor men (known to be Republicans) to club together in order to buy a building lot assessed at something above £100. After the deed had been recorded, showing them as joint owners, he instructed one of them to go and register as a qualified voter. On another day, the second joint owner registered. Then the third. So, a precedent was established. After that, several groups of men — known Republicans — qualified and registered. Perhaps they even borrowed the money in order to purchase real estate from the Bank of the Manhattan Company!

By this relatively simple and quite legal process, many Republican names were added to the voting lists. The property qualifications for voters became a dead letter.

As a consequence, although the Federalists had elected John Jay as governor of New York in 1799, the Democratic-Republicans were victorious in New York in the election of 1800. And it was the block of Republican votes from New York that decided the national election of 1800 — the election of Jefferson and Burr. Here was the material for further antagonism between Burr and Hamilton. (And, unfortunately, between Burr and Jefferson.)

During the political campaign preceding the national election of 1800, a very peculiar thing happened. Beyond any doubt, it served to heighten the already existing tension between Burr and Hamilton. It may have been a major step in the series of events which culminated in the duel, four years later.

There was no secret about the fact that Hamilton had no liking and little respect for Pres. John Adams. During all of the first three years of the Adams administration, Hamilton managed to exert a considerable degree of personal influence in the president's cabinet and among the members of the Federalist majority in Congress. Finally,

9

Adams became aware that Hamilton was operating behind the scenes in ways which undermined the president's position. When he did become convinced that strings were being pulled, he proceeded to cut them. He made three changes in his cabinet and he directed other changes in personnel, in high places.

No matter what his personal feelings were, Hamilton could not prevent the renomination of Adams for another term as president. This time, Charles Cotesworth Pinckney was chosen to be Adams' "running mate," rather than Thomas Pinckney (these two men were brothers, from South Carolina).

This was before the adoption of the Twelfth Amendment to the United States Constitution. Hamilton saw that if the Federalists were to win the national election, it would be possible for him to influence or to manipulate the electoral vote so that Pinckney would become president and Adams would be relegated to the vice-presidency again. Persuading only one or two Federalist electors to vote for Pinckney and for someone other than Adams would accomplish this.

With this end clearly in view, Hamilton wrote a pamphlet assailing the Adams administration in general and Pres. John Adams in particular. It was a classic example of party disloyalty. Its language was intemperate. For example: it stated that Adams was guilty of "disgusting egotism, distempered jealousy, and ungovernable indiscretion." It said of the president that there were "great and intrinsic defects in his character which make him unfit for the office of Chief Magistrate."

Not only did Hamilton write this pamphlet; he had it published (a limited edition) over his signature. Of course, the pamphlet was intended to reach only a certain circle of selected Federalists. But, by some unexpected process, one or more copies reached the desk of Col. Aaron Burr. He immediately saw that it could serve as a powerful factor in support of the Democratic-Republican cause. He sent it to the editor of the New York *Aurora* and to the editor of the New London *Bee*. It was copied from these by other papers.

The results of the publication of Hamilton's attack upon Adams were sensational. Adams fumed. Hamilton squirmed. Many Federalists were shocked. Many Republicans were amused. And, Hamilton determined that he would oppose, even more strongly than ever before, any possible political advancement for Colonel Burr — or any advancement in any field, for that matter.

There was another aspect of this matter of Hamilton's unofficial and unauthorized meddling in the affairs of the Adams administration. Although it did not directly affect Burr or the Burr-Hamilton relationship, it certainly added to the tensions under which the ex-secretary of the treasury lived and worked. When he found that it was not possible for him to affect American foreign policy according to his personal desires by means of his secret pressures upon the secretary of state, he used a direct approach to the situation. He became his Britannic majesty's "Agent Number 7." Of course this was known to the British minister to the United States but apparently it was not known to any leader of American politics at that time.[6]

Hamilton was aware of Burr's amazing ability to become informed about political and diplomatic developments which were not publicized. It is reasonable to assume that he felt a certain amount of apprehension, lest Colonel Burr become cognizant of his attempt to direct the course of

---

6 Actually, this was not made known in the United States until 1964. See publication by Julian P. Boyd: "Number 7."

American-British relations by means of a secret and direct approach.

The Republicans won the election of 1800, so neither Adams nor Pinckney could become president in 1801. Jefferson and Burr each received seventy-three electoral votes and the "old" House of Representatives, where Hamilton still had some influence, chose Jefferson for the presidency. Burr became vice-president.[7]

Some writers have raised the rather academic question: "Would Burr have accepted the presidency in 1801, if the House had elected him rather than Jefferson?" The question may be viewed in this light:

One American statesman (Henry Clay) said: "I would rather be right than be president" and a few American leaders have stated that they have had no desire to serve in the presidency. But no man who has been elected to the highest office in the nation ever has refused to serve and no vice-president ever has indicated that he would refuse to serve, if his chief were to be removed from the high office by death or by other means. Who, in the political field, would not be pleased to serve as the president of the United States?

It also is true that some writers have insinuated that Colonel Burr tried to secure the presidency, when the House was voting in 1801. This certainly was not the case. If Burr had been willing to make a deal with the Federalists, he would have been selected for the first position, on one of the early ballots and the week-long process of repeated ballots would have been avoided. As a matter of fact, it was Jefferson who finally indicated that he would not

---

7 The presidential elections of 1796 and 1800 were very close contests. In 1796, the electoral vote was: Adams, 71; Jefferson, 68; T. Pinckney, 59; Burr, 30; the other votes were widely scattered. In 1800, the electoral vote was Jefferson, 73; Burr, 73; Adams, 65; C.C. Pinckney, 64; Jay, 1.

12

make any sweeping changes in government personnel, if he were elected.[8]

It is a fact that Burr was to be accused of some type of party disloyalty, at a later date. In order to observe and to celebrate the birthday of George Washington, on February 22, 1802, a great banquet was held in the nation's capital city. This affair was arranged by prominent Federalists and Federalists were in the majority among those who attended. But by 1802, the first president had become more than a party symbol: already he was acclaimed as "The Father of his Country," by men of varying political beliefs. As a consequence, there were some Republicans among the Federalists at the banquet. And through the personal influence of Senator Bayard of Delaware, Vice-President Burr was present as the guest of honor. When the vice-president was called upon to propose a toast, he rose in his place, held his glass aloft and said, in clear, ringing tones that all could hear: "To the Union of All Honest Men!" There was silence as the toast was drunk — silence followed by a buzz of excited conversation. What did the vice-president mean by "The Union of All Honest Men?"

The immediate and obvious interpretation of the toast was that it repeated or echoed what Jefferson had said in his inaugural address, almost two years previously. Jefferson had asserted: "We are all Republicans: we are all Federalists." At that time, his statement had been accepted as a declaration of national unity which was above party divisions. Now, however, when the same sentiment was expressed by Burr, in only slightly different terms, his enemies pounced upon it and said that it was an indica-

---

8 Colonel Burr remained in Albany while the balloting was in process. Mr. Jefferson was in Washington and was in daily consultation with party leaders.

tion that he was seeking Federalist support for his own political advancement. They expressed the opinion that he was being disloyal to the principles of the Republican party.

Jefferson had served as vice-president of the United States during the four years of the John Adams administration. During that time, he had been neglected and pushed aside by the president. This was to be expected because the two men were political opposites. They were leaders of opposing parties and they had divergent points of view.

From March 1801 until January 1805, President Jefferson treated Vice-President Burr just as he had been treated while he held the vice-presidential office. Burr was neglected and pushed aside. But this should not have been the case. The circumstances were not the same in the two cases. Jefferson and Burr were in the same political fold. And it had been Burr who had carried the pivotal state of New York into the Democratic-Republican column in the national election of 1800. Yet, none of Burr's lieutenants and supporters had received any political reward. Other New Yorkers were singled out for preferment by Jefferson.

It was not until Burr's term as vice-president was drawing to a close (and, incidentally, after the duel with Hamilton), in January and February of 1805, that Jefferson began to show any marks of favor to Burr and the Burrites. This belated recognition was due to the fact that the vice-president (as president of the Senate) would preside over the impeachment trial of Associate Justice Samuel Chase of the United States Supreme Court. Jefferson very much desired that Chase should be found guilty and removed from the bench. But Burr conducted an eminently fair and proper trial, with the result that the impeachment charges did not carry and the president's attempt to bring

14

the Court under the control of the chief executive was thwarted.[9]

As a direct result of Jefferson's highly questionable tactics, Burr's political "machine" in New York had crumbled. In addition to that he was to be replaced by George Clinton in the vice-presidency. Nor was he to be offered any place of honor or position in the second Jefferson administration. Jefferson had decided that Burr was not to be offered a Cabinet post, nor was he to be appointed to serve as a minister to any foreign country. Neither was he to be placed on the Supreme Court or to be made a brigadier in the army. Insofar as Jefferson was concerned, Aaron Burr was to become a private citizen on March 4, 1805 and as such, he could make and take a place for himself.[10]

In order to meet this situation in a positive manner and in order to restore his own political status in his home state, Burr became an "independent" candidate for governor, of New York. His opponent was the "regular" Republican, Judge Morgan Lewis.[11] The moribund Federalist party did not present a candidate in this gubernatorial contest.

The campaign was a particularly bitter, vindictive, spiteful and destructive one. Burr carried the city of New

---

9 For a presentation of the trial of Assoc. Justice Chase, see: "A. Burr: Historians' Foil," by Samuel Engle Burr, Jr., *The Lodestar*, The American University, Washington, D.C., Summer issue, 1965. Vol. X, No. 2, pp. 5 — 10, illustrated.

10 Jefferson kept a diary (The Anas) in which he recorded his various activities, over a period of years. He lived a long life (1743-1826) and after his retirement, he had the time and the opportunity to revise, rewrite and edit "The Anas" in accordance with his "hindsight," so that they would present those matters which he wanted to be retained and so that they would present that personal bias or slant which he wanted to perpetuate.

11 Morgan Lewis was a classmate of Aaron Burr (class of 1772) at the College of New Jersey (Princeton). Another member of that class was James Madison.

York and several nearby counties by small majorities but Lewis secured larger majorities in the upstate counties. The result was the election of Lewis by a three to two majority. This ended Aaron Burr's active political career.

Some further light on the personality of Colonel Burr may be secured by considering his beliefs in philosophy and in religion. Col. Aaron Burr became a Stoic in his philosophy and a Deist in his religious belief.

The major elements in the Stoic philosophy may be stated as follows:

Good and evil are relative concepts rather than absolutes. Misfortunes in the lives of men are incidents in a totality, to be weighed with fortunate and neutral incidents. The life of each man must be considered in relationship to the lives of his contemporaries. Man must accept the past as factual but he can plan and work and strive in the present and for the future. However, once an event has been recorded it cannot be changed but it may be accorded a place of more or of less importance in his thinking. "That which has been" and "That which now is" must be recognized and accepted but life is in the present, not in the past. Happiness for man, in this earthly existence, is to be attained by having man adjust his thinking and his behavior to an acceptance of facts and to the cosmic forces which operate beyond his control.

The major parts of the Deistic point of view may be summarized in this way:

God created the universe and God continues to exist. He exists without any personal type of relationship to the creatures in his creation. There is no conflict between God and science. Science deals with the laws of God, as they continue to operate and to function. The order and harmony which are apparent in the overall workings of the universe are due to the nature of God's work as the creator. Reason, rather than revelation, is the key to an understanding of God. Man can understand God only partially or imperfectly because of the greatness of God and of the relatively lesser position of man in the totality which has been brought into being. Man acts in accordance with the general plan of God but man does have some limited amount of free will. He does have the power to make many choices — within the limits of his nature.[12]

---

[12] Colonel Burr was not completely Deistic in his beliefs, however. He did believe in the power and efficacy of prayer. Frequently, after clients or friends had received advice or counsel from him, he said, as they left his office, "And I shall remember you in my prayers."

Part II: The Duel:
The Tragic Duel

THERE HAVE BEEN historians and other writers who have maintained that Hamilton was opposed to taking human life, or even opposed to placing human life in jeopardy. This has been ascribed to his beliefs "as a Christian," or on strictly moral grounds. The evidence at hand does not support such a position.

Hamilton served as an officer in the army of the American Revolution when thousands of lives were at stake and when many lives were lost. He gave up his desk job as an aide to General Washington, so that he could go into the field, at Yorktown. He did this so that he would be able to say, in later years, that he had been actively engaged in the blood and thunder of an actual battle with the enemy.

Later, when Hamilton had attained a general's rank, he wanted to conduct a bloody purge of the Maryland and Pennsylvania farmers, during the "Whiskey Rebellion."

18

Again, he wanted to be personally involved in the blood-letting.

Hamilton's brother-in-law, John Barker Church, was a duelist. His brace of dueling pistols (which did not conform to the "code") had been used a number of times before the Burr-Hamilton encounter.

Hamilton's oldest son, Philip Schuyler Hamilton, was killed in a duel with George I. Eaker, at Weehawken, in 1801.

Hamilton had issued a definite challenge to a duel in 1795. The man whom he challenged was Commo. James Nicholson, the father-in-law of Albert Gallatin. The place mentioned was Pawlus Hook and the confrontation was to take place on the Monday after the challenge was issued (July 20, 1795). He asked Col. Nicholas Fish to act as his second. Colonel Fish succeeded in securing from the commodore a statement to the effect that "he had no memory of having made the rude and insulting remarks attributed to him by General Hamilton." Consequently, the "affair of honor" was avoided.

And, there was the situation which involved Hamilton and James Monroe. It grew out of the disclosures of the Reynolds affair and the questions about Hamilton's financial operations. In July and August, 1797, Monroe construed statements in letters to him, from Hamilton, as a challenge. He indicated that he would accept the challenge and he asked his friend, Col. Aaron Burr, to act as his second. Others who were involved in this matter were John Barker Church (for Hamilton) and David Gelston (for Monroe). It was Burr who was able to prevent this duel and to arrange a peaceful settlement between the two principals. In view of what was to happen in 1804, this situation is one of the ironies of history.[1]

---

[1] It is reported that Mrs. Hamilton never forgave Monroe and that she refused to speak to him, thereafter.

During the campaign for the governorship of New York in 1804, the culminating element in the Burr-Hamilton antagonism developed. It was the verbal and written vilification of Burr by Hamilton. Some of it got into the public press and it was used as the specific matter which brought about that unfortunate encounter, the duel between these two men.

The correspondence about this has been preserved and has been published in full.[2]

The book on the duel presents an introductory statement, the correspondence, and an epilogue. The correspondence speaks for itself. The epilogue contains one unfortunate reference to "treasonous involvement." (Page 174) This reference to treason should be looked upon as a biased statement.

From the correspondence, these facts are evident: (1) the matter started with a statement by General Hamilton which was published in the public press; (2) Colonel Burr requested an explanation; (3) General Hamilton procrastinated and evaded the issue, by trying to divert the train of thought; (4) After an exchange of several letters, Colonel Burr challenged; (5) General Hamilton accepted the challenge.

General Hamilton did not need to prolong the exchange of correspondence with Colonel Burr as he did. Neither did he need to be obtuse and evasive in his letters. And, rather than to accept the challenge when it finally came, he could have declined to meet Colonel Burr on "the field of honor." In that era, not all challenges were accepted, even between "gentlemen." He could have made an explanation, as he

---

2 "Interview in Weehawken" by Harold C. Syrett and Jean G. Cook, (editors), Middletown, Conn., Wesleyan University Press, 1960.

did in the Reynolds case. He could have made an apology.[3] There were legitimate ways in which he could have prevented the meeting at Weehawken. He decided not to use them. So, the final responsibility for the duel rested with General Hamilton rather than with Colonel Burr.

The date that was chosen for the Burr-Hamilton encounter was July 11, 1804. On the morning of that day, Colonel Burr and his second, Mr. Van Ness, went to the dueling ground at Weehawken. Also, General Hamilton, Judge Pendleton and Dr. Hosack went to the appointed

---

[3] The best example of this procedure, in American history, came nearly half a century later when Jefferson Davis refused to accept a challenge from Judah P. Benjamin. He issued an apology and soon afterward he appointed Benjamin to a position in the Confederate cabinet. Also, Gen. Andrew Jackson challenged Gen. Winfield Scott. Scott refused to meet him "on the field of honor," saying that for the time being Jackson might consider him a coward but that such an opinion would be false. "Wait for the next war to determine if I am a coward," he is reported to have said. The two men spoke to one another politely, after this episode.

It is true, also, that another American political leader avoided a duel by means of an "agreement."

Abraham Lincoln almost became involved in a duel, in the fall of 1842. The challenging party was James Shields, another attorney. The place was to have been a spot in Missouri, opposite Alton, Illinois. The weapons were to have been broadswords. Gen. James D. Whiteside was chosen by Shields to act as his second. Lincoln selected Dr. E. H. Merryman as his second. Lincoln, with his second, and Shields, with his second, were rowed in two separate boats, to a sandbar on the Missouri side of the Mississippi River. Several interested gentlemen accompanied them. While the seconds conferred, Lincoln strode back and forth, brandishing one of the swords. He was a full foot taller than Shields and had correspondingly longer arms, so that his choice of weapons gave him a distinct advantage. The conference of the seconds resulted in a "full and satisfactory" agreement which was accepted by both of the principals. (The argument had developed as a result of the publication of the "Rebecca" letters in the Sangamon *Journal*.) The two principals then were rowed back to the Illinois shore in the same boat, talking in a friendly manner with one another during the process. This was on September 22, 1842. Lincoln advanced in his political career to become president of the United States. Shields served in the Union army during the War of 1861-1865, attaining the rank of major general (with Lincoln's approval). Later, he served in the United States Senate, first as a senator from Illinois and later as a senator from Minnesota.

place. All of these men went voluntarily — no one forced anyone else to go.

There is no historical record to indicate that Colonel Burr was an expert marksman with the pistol. His weapon as an army officer had been the sword — not the pistol or the rifle. The story that he engaged in target practice at Richmond Hill on the day before the duel (with a cherry tree as the target) is a pure fabrication, with an obvious anti-Burr purpose.

The duel was conducted in full accord with the accepted code of that day. Every detail of the code was observed, meticulously. The only unusual element was that General Hamilton asked for time to adjust his spectacles, to assist in sighting his pistol.

The pistols were supplied by General Hamilton. They were the property of his brother-in-law, John Barker Church, and they were of heavier caliber than the limit set in the code.

Each principal (or more probably the seconds, acting for them) had reserved a barge and several bargemen to row it across the river. General Hamilton also had arranged for a physician (Dr. David Hosack) to accompany him as far as the landing place below the Palisades. All of this arranging was done voluntarily and deliberately, with no force or pressuring being applied to any of the persons concerned.

After the duel, General Hamilton was taken back to New York in the rowboat which he had rented. By that time, there was bright sunshine on the river. He was carried to the William Bayard house[4] and his family was summoned.

---

4 William Bayard was a member of the firm of LeRoy, Bayard and McEvers, merchants in New York City. Hamilton had served as their attorney from time to time.

This Mr. Bayard should not be confused with Sen. James A. Bayard of Delaware. Although a Federalist in politics, Senator Bayard was a personal friend of Colonel Burr.

22

There was no attempt at surgery and the only medical care was the administration of opium (or laudanum) to lessen his pain.

Hamilton's wound was a peculiar one. It certainly was not the type of wound which was intended to be fatal — it was not in the head and not near the heart. The bullet entered Hamilton's right side, struck the bottom rib and was deflected upward, through the liver. It lodged near the spine. If it had been a fraction of an inch lower, or if it had not been deflected as it was, it might have done relatively little harm. The place where the bullet struck Hamilton would indicate that Colonel Burr wanted him to experience some pain and suffering but that he did not plan to kill his opponent.

General Hamilton died about thirty-six hours after he had been shot — very likely from loss of blood and various complications. This was on July 12, 1804.

As soon as news of the duel became known, controversy arose about it. It was rumored that there had been secret eyewitnesses to the event — that several persons had arrived early at the dueling grounds and had hidden in the underbrush. These stories appear to be pure fabrications. Only four persons are known to have been present, the two principals and the two seconds: Colonel Burr, General Hamilton, Mr. Van Ness and Judge Pendleton. Dr. Hosack had remained near the boats, at the riverbank.

There is no doubt but that Colonel Burr fired his pistol and that the bullet hit General Hamilton, just at the base of the ribs, on the right side.

There are at least four stories about General Hamilton's "first fire." (1) He took aim, fired at Colonel Burr and missed his mark. (2) At the command, he fired, aiming above Colonel Burr's head. (3) He fired aimlessly and perhaps involuntarily when his opponent's bullet entered his side. (4) He did not fire at all.

23

Those who incline favorably toward the cause of Colonel Burr are likely to accept the first version. Those who favor General Hamilton are sure to select one of the other stories.

On the afternoon of July 11 (the day of the duel), the Episcopal bishop of New York, the Rt. Rev. Benjamin Moore, was summoned to Hamilton's bedside. It then developed that, for all of his pious utterances about being a Christian and about having Christian scruples against dueling, there was some doubt about Hamilton's baptism and confirmation. And even if he were in good standing in the church, there was some doubt about the propriety of administering the sacrament of the Holy Eucharist to one who had willfully participated in a duel. After due consideration, the bishop decided that he should not administer the rite and he departed.

Then, a clergyman of the Dutch Reformed Church, Dr. Mason, was asked to conduct a communion service, in the bedroom, for the dying man. He also decided that such a procedure would be improper and he refused. But, toward evening, Bishop Moore returned to the sickroom. He said that he had reconsidered his previous decision and he did conduct an abbreviated service, administering the sacrament to the fallen leader, in the presence of his wife and their children.[5]

Hamilton left a number of papers which he had prepared especially for use in case of his death. A letter addressed to Timothy Sedgwick dealt with political matters, with particular reference to the value of maintaining the federal union. There was a letter to his wife, imploring her continued esteem for him, and reminding her that she might

---

[5] Bishop Moore's wife was a cousin of Mrs. Theodosia Bartow Burr, the first wife of Col. Aaron Burr. Both Mrs. Moore and Mrs. Burr were descendants of the Reverend John Bartow, rector of the first Anglican parish in Westchester County, New York.

derive great comfort from her religion.[6] Another letter was on the subject of care for his aunt (or cousin), Mrs. Ann Mitchell.

During the period of time that had elapsed between the challenge (June 27) and the duel (July 11), Colonel Burr did some paperwork, too. He wrote a new will and he wrote two letters: one addressed to his daughter, Theoddosia, and one to his son-in-law, Joseph Alston. These letters were not destroyed after the duel. They have been published.

When compared with the amount of material written by Hamilton just before the "affair," the Burr material is much less in volume. For the writers of history and hence for the readers of history, the letters of the man who died have had greater emotional appeal than have the letters of the man who lived.

---

[6] The letter to Hamilton's wife has been used by various writers as a means for building up the "martyr" position or complex, which very likely is what Hamilton desired.

Part III: Aftermath

The Apotheosis of General Hamilton
The Vilification of Colonel Burr

D URING THE TIME that General Hamilton lay on his deathbed (a period of thirty-six hours) a tremendous change took place in his status: in the public press, in the pulpit, and in the personal opinions of many American citizens. Overnight, his faults seemed to be forgotten and his virtues seemed to be magnified.

No longer did Hamilton stand forth as the advocate of an American aristocracy. His designation of the general public (the common man) as "that great beast" was relegated to the background. He no longer was Adams' detractor or the self-appointed quasi-leader of a dying political party. Once again, he became the architect of the new national economy and the creator of a firm and stable financial basis for the nation.

On the other hand, Colonel Burr, who had been known

as the friend of "the man in the street" now was denounced by those whom he had befriended. Only a few months before the duel, he had received more than forty percent of the votes cast for governor of New York. Now, he was execrated by a great majority of the people — people who knew little of the reasons for the duel and who had received garbled accounts of the circumstances surrounding it.

Colonel Burr was indicted for a misdemeanor (issuing a challenge) in New York (where both he and Hamilton had written their correspondence) and for murder, in New Jersey, where the duel had taken place.[1]

Such legal actions were unprecedented. Challenges were issued and duels were fought fairly frequently in the 1700s and the early 1800s and charges were not brought against the principals or their seconds. (See Part V.)

Because of the unusual furor and excitement, Colonel Burr left New York and traveled to Georgia, stopping at Perth Amboy and Cranbury, New Jersey, Philadelphia, Washington and Charleston. He made a brief visit to Spanish Florida and then went to his daughter's home in South Carolina. When Congress reconvened, he was back in Washington where he presided over the meetings of the United States Senate. But Richmond Hill, his beautiful home in New York City, had to be sold (with all its furnishings) at a price far below its actual value, in order to meet the insistent demands of certain creditors.

General Hamilton was buried in Trinity Churchyard in New York City, with a funeral parade, full military honors and much oratory. His friends sponsored a plan whereby gifts were made to prevent his family from being in debt. After all of his financial obligations had been met, there was a balance of about $25,000 for his widow and children.

---

[1] These charges were never pressed and Colonel Burr never was arrested on either of these indictments.

There also was the house, called "Hamilton Grange" and a bit of land surrounding it. And, as a member of the wealthy Schuyler family, Elizabeth Hamilton had considerable financial backing, in her own right.

After his term as vice-president ended on March 4, 1805, Colonel Burr turned his attention to the West. Even before this time he had been interested in certain tracts of land in western New York and in Ohio. Now his attention was directed still further west. It should be remembered that Kentucky and Tennessee had become states while he was serving as a member of the United States Senate. And Ohio had been admitted to the Union while he had been vice-president. And there was Louisiana — the purchase of that vast area was accomplished in the same year that Ohio attained statehood, 1803.

The Louisiana Purchase was negotiated by means of a treaty between the United States and the Empire of France (Napoleon I) while Colonel Burr was serving as vice-president and as the presiding officer of the U.S. Senate. The proposed treaty was placed before the Senate on October 17 and was approved on October 25, 1803. This transaction served to extend and to expand Colonel Burr's already formed mind-set for the attainment of future fame and fortune by means of dealing in real estate on a grand scale.

Because he had served as attorney general of the state of New York, he also had served (ex officio) as a commissioner of public lands for the state. Further than that, he had made personal investments in real estate by buying large blocks of stock in the Holland Land Company and other companies. The Holland Land Company had large holdings of undeveloped acreage in western New York and in parts of Ohio.

Now that the vast area of the Louisiana Purchase was to be American, Colonel Burr began to take an interest

28

in the Bastrop Grant and he looked further afield toward Mexico, the Floridas, the Bahamas, the Bermudas, and western Canada as possible areas for conquest, settlement, and development.[2]

Colonel Burr conferred with the Hon. Anthony Merry, minister from England, regarding freeing Mexico and/or the Floridas from Spain and with the Marquis, Don Carlos Martinez de Yrujo, minister from Spain, regarding freeing some parts of British North America from Great Britain.

He found that the British government would not provide him with any assistance in any proposed attempt to free the Spanish possessions from Spain and that Spain had no interest in the fate of the remaining British colonies in North America. If he was to secure powerful backing for any plan of liberation, it would have to come from some other source — not from Great Britain and not from Spain.[3]

Colonel Burr was not the only person who discussed his plans with the British minister. Mr. Merry made mention of a variety of so-called "schemes" in his reports to London.

---

2 General Hamilton also speculated in land values. At the time when the location of the new District of Columbia was being determined, he acquired title to a considerable acreage just north of the new capital. (The present area of Glen Echo Heights, Mohican Hills and Tulip Hill.)

3 It is reported that in the British archives there are several letters from Mr. Merry concerning Colonel Burr. These are quoted as saying that Colonel Burr had offered to "revolutionize" the western country and to separate this area from the federal Union. The areas of chief concern in this were the states of Kentucky and Tennessee and the territory of Mississippi. Such a report must be evaluated in terms of Mr. Merry's political desires and his assessment of the Jefferson administration. Mr. Merry was notoriously disenchanted with the national administration. He did not think highly of Mr. Jefferson or of his policies in the field of international politics. There is no reliable evidence to indicate that Colonel Burr ever suggested that the western country could be detached from the Union. As a matter of fact, Mr. Merry's communication to his government frequently reflected his own personal sentiments and desires. Nor were they always consistent with his own reports made at an earlier date. Reports made to the British government by Charles A. Williamson certainly differed — regarding Colonel Burr's proposals — from those made by Mr. Merry.

But most historians have been selective. They have adhered to the "concensus" which treated Colonel Burr's activities in a different way. They have referred to Colonel Burr's talks with Mr. Merry while they have said little or nothing about what others may have confided to Mr. Merry.[4]

It also should be mentioned that Colonel Burr had one or more conferences with the filibuster leader, General Francisco de Miranda. Miranda was organizing an expedition designed to achieve independence for Venezuela. Colonel Burr felt that Miranda lacked the backing that he would require in order to be successful — and this proved to be the case.

After a preliminary trip down the Ohio and Mississippi rivers from Pittsburg to New Orleans, Colonel Burr organized his famous Expedition to the West. The two related purposes were: (1) to colonize a tract of half a million acres of land on the Ouachita River[5] (half of the Baron Bastrop Grant); and (2) to be ready to lead American volunteers into Mexico when the "inevitable" war with Spain would begin. Everyone (even President Jefferson) expected that such a war would break out at almost any moment.

But President Jefferson was determined that Colonel Burr never should be allowed an opportunity to hold any position of political prominence again. He issued a presidential proclamation at the end of November, 1806. In it, he condemned the Burr Expedition and indicated that in

---

4 In connection with Colonel Burr's contacts with the British minister to the United States and with several other British statesmen, see: "Britain and the Aaron Burr Conspiracy," by Raymond A. Mohl, in *History Today,* (London), issue dated June 1971, pp. 391-398. Vol. XXI, No. 6.

5 This area was to become the new state of Burrsylvania, with the capital city to be named Theodosia. Colonel Burr would serve as its first governor and later as one of its senators in Washington. This is Burr family tradition, lacking any known written basis.

some obscure or mysterious and devious manner, treason against the United States was involved. A warrant was issued for Colonel Burr's arrest.[6]

Jefferson's action in issuing a presidential proclamation against the Burr Expedition to the West was for purely political purposes. He wanted to make it impossible for Colonel Burr to regain a position of national power or political prominence. An indication of this is the fact that no proclamations were issued against other privately organized expeditions to the western lands. Some of them involved many more persons than did the Burr Expedition, but none of their leaders were accused of treason. Some of the leaders of other expeditions were: Philip Nolan,[7] Dr. James D. Long, Hayden Edwards, Peter Ellis Bean, Moses Austin, Stephen F. Austin, Green DeWitt, Sterling C. Robertson, and Augustus Magee. None of these men posed any threat to the continuation of the Virginia dynasty of presidents, which Jefferson wanted to insure.

Most of these leaders were quite indefinite as to the lands to which they were going — they intended to seize what they wanted, when they saw western land that pleased them. The Austins and Colonel Burr (and perhaps a few others) arranged in advance as to the land which they intended to colonize.

Hayden Edwards led a group of United States citizens

---

6 Some individuals and groups have seen fit to call The Burr Expedition to the West by this name: "The Burr-Blennerhassett Insurrection." The use of this misleading term is an apparent attempt to justify the fact that the local militia was sent to Blennerhassett Island, where they caused a great amount of damage.

7 It should be noted that there was a real Philip Nolan. Unfortunately, Edward Everett Hale used this name (and Colonel Burr's name) in his short story: "The Man Without a Country," which is pure fiction. It was written in 1863 as a means of stirring up patriotic feeling in the North, during the War Between the States.

to the vicinity of Nacogdoches, in East Texas.[8] In 1826, he proclaimed "The Republic of Fredonia," with indefinite boundaries. He certainly included Mexican territory in it and perhaps parts of Louisiana, also. He raised a red and white flag as the emblem of his new nation. Its slogan or motto was: "Independence, Liberty, & Justice."[9]

The Republic of Fredonia had a short life. It came to an end when the Mexican government sent a body of troops to suppress it. A few Fredonians were killed and most of the others returned to the United States.

But no one in the United States was ready to charge Edwards with "treasonous activities," while all of this was taking place — or afterward, either. Yet it was clear that he was attempting to seize and to govern territory which was within the accepted boundary of a "friendly nation," and perhaps some United States territory, along with it.

It is estimated that as many as 3,000 men were involved in the Gutiérrez-Magee-Kemper Expedition of 1812 and that about 1,000 of them volunteered or were recruited in the United States.[10] The Long Expedition of 1819 involved about 300 men. It was organized in the southwest and left from Natchez. This group invaded Texas and proclaimed an independent republic with Dr. Long as president. More American recruits were secured in 1820 and in 1821 but in spite of this, the "republic" soon came to an end.

---

8 Haden Edwards (also spelled Hayden) was born in Stafford County, Virginia, on August 12, 1771. It appears that he was not a descendant of the Reverend Jonathan Edwards of Massachusetts. Some years after his ill-fated "Republic" collapsed, he returned to Texas and died at Nacogdoches in 1849. His son, Haden H. Edwards (1813-1865) was prominent in the military and political history of the Republic of Texas.

9 It really was his brother, Benjamin W. Edwards, who issued the Fredonian "Declaration of Independence." In this, he was joined by two other Americans: Richard Fields and Dr. John D. Hunter.

10 This was the "Green Flag Republic." See: *Green Flag Over Texas*, by Julia Kathryn Garrett; Austin, Texas, The Pemberton Press, 1969.

The government of the United States made no protests, issued no proclamations and took no action in the cases of these expeditions.

During the course of the double decade from 1805 to 1825, as many as thirty American citizens organized and led private "Expeditions to the West." But Colonel Burr was the only leader of such an expedition to be pursued, arrested, prosecuted and persecuted by the national administration.

A few leaders of expeditions to the West were arrested and imprisoned — but by Spanish or Mexican authorities — not by American authorities.

When the Burr Expedition reached the vicinity of Natchez, Mississippi (Bayou Pierre), Colonel Burr was arrested and his followers were ordered to disband.[11].

There were from ninety to one hundred persons in the Burr Expedition, some fifteen or twenty of them being women and children. Their only arms were those which any group would need when going into the wilderness.

The charges against Colonel Burr had no foundation in fact and no incriminating evidence was produced in court. Even so, the charges were not dismissed and he was required

---

11 Some of the correspondence concerning the Burr Expedition to the West was conducted in code and Colonel Burr has been criticized by some of his detractors because of this. Such adverse criticism is quite unwarranted. At this period of time, many prominent men (and also some who were less prominent) used codes or ciphers. Sometimes, these men invented or contrived their own personal ciphers while they were students in college and then used them throughout the entire span of their lives. Many agents who carried mail were likely to read the letters which they handled. The code or cipher served to conceal or to distort the real meaning of the material which they read. It was a means for securing privacy in correspondence. In August, 1949, a dealer in rare books and autographs (Goodspeed's, Boston) offered for sale a two-page document dated March 1, 1784, explaining "one of Jefferson's codes," and bearing his initials. At that time, the price quoted for this Jeffersonian document was $215. Benjamin Franklin, who was a colonial postmaster general, sometimes used not only a code but also a rebus pattern in certain correspondence, as a means of confusing any casual reader of his letters.

to appear in court, at Natchez or at Washington, Mississippi, day after day. In order to escape from this situation and also in order to escape from armed agents sent from New Orleans to seize him, he started eastward on horseback, with one companion. Again he was arrested by federal agents. This time, he was escorted — under armed guard — to Richmond, Virginia, to be tried for treason.

The presiding judge at his trial was John Marshall, chief justice of the United States. After months of legal proceedings, a verdict of "not guilty" was reached. It was recorded on October 19, 1807.

Also, Harman Blennerhassett, who had been associated with Colonel Burr in the "Expedition to the West," had been charged with treason, had been arrested and was placed on trial. He, too, was found "not guilty."

During all of the time from November, 1806 until October, 1807 — for practically a full year, the writers of articles and pamphlets had been fulminating against Colonel Burr. All of his plans were called plots, schemes or conspiracies.[12] All of his acts were labeled as subversive.

Even though the whole weight of the federal government had been thrown against him with no success, and he had not been found guilty of any crime, the public mind had been alienated, poisoned and inflamed.

---

12 The American public was so misinformed, so misled, so influenced against Colonel Burr by vindictive politicians, "yellow" journalists and paid pamphleteers that even a full century later, a writer who was not anti-Burr considered it necessary to refer to the Burr Expedition as a "conspiracy." This writer was Walter F. McCaleb whose book had the title: "The Aaron Burr Conspiracy," (published 1903, expanded and republished, 1936). As a matter of fact, Dr. McCaleb's book proved to be favorable to the cause of Colonel Burr. Of course, the detractors, the enemies of Colonel Burr, especially the Jeffersonians, always labeled the expedition as the "conspiracy," using that "smear" word with all possible frequency and emphasis.

He decided to go to Europe. After visits to England, Scotland, Sweden, Denmark and several of the German principalities (dukedoms), he went to Paris and suggested to Napoleon that he (Colonel Burr) should lead French troops in liberating Mexico from Spain. In his proposals to the emperor, he mentioned other Spanish colonies (Florida, etc.) and some British ones, too (the Bahamas, etc.) but the emphasis was on Mexico.[13]

Failing to get a favorable hearing from Napoleon, he decided that he should return to New York and resume the practice of law. It seemed to be a reasonable decision. His daughter had urged him to adopt such a plan. But returning to New York was not such an easy matter. Both the American representatives in France and the agents of the imperial government of France contrived to delay his departure for almost two years. Finally, the necessary papers were secured. Passage was booked on a Dutch ship, sailing from Amsterdam. He paid exorbitant fees to have a cabin set aside and fitted up in proper style for him. Late in September, the ship sailed.

On September 29, 1811 the British frigate *La Desirée* captured the Dutch vessel and took it as a prize of war to England, with its passengers and crew.

Now the whole process of securing a passport and visa and of finding a suitable ship for the trip to America had to be repeated. It was not until March 26, 1812 that Colonel Burr was able to leave England, en route to America. He had to use an assumed name and to take passage to Boston rather than to New York. He chose to be M. Alolphus Arnot. M. Arnot was an alert, polite, well-dressed gentle-

---

[13] Fifty years later (1863), Emperor Napoleon III made use of Colonel Burr's plans by sending 5,000 French troops to establish the Archduke Maximilian as the emperor of Mexico. See: *Napoleon's Dossier on Aaron Burr*, by Samuel Engle Burr, Jr., San Antonio, Texas, The Naylor Company, 1969.

man of middle age, with a mustache and goatee, who spoke only French, but whose eighteen pieces of baggage and luggage were boldly labeled "A.B."

The ship which brought him to America was the *Aurora*, (Captain Potter), of Newburyport. It arrived at Boston on May 4, 1812.

Part IV: Home Again:
A Career in Law

ON JUNE 7, 1808, Col. Aaron Burr went on board the packet *Clarissa Ann* at New York en route to England. On June 8, 1812, Col. Aaron Burr resumed the practice of law at 9 Nassau Street, New York. He had been away from the city for precisely four years.[1]

For the next twenty-four years, he was busy at his profession. Once again, he was one of the leading lawyers of the city and the state. He needed associates and assistants to work with him and he found a number of young lawyers who wished to be associated with him. Some of the lawyers who were his partners, associates or assistants from time to time were: Col. William D. Craft, G. W. Lathrop, Esq., M. H. Flandrau, Esq., Nelson Chase, Esq., and John Pelle-

---

[1] Colonel Burr (or M. Arnot) was able to arrange for his trip from England to the United States just in the nick of time. Any further delay would have amounted to a disaster. President Madison sent his war message to Congress on June 1, and Congress declared war on Great Britain on June 18, 1812.

treau, Esq. (Incidentally, Mr. Chase was the husband of Mme. Jumel's adopted daughter.)

Perhaps his most famous case during this period was that involving the Mecdef Eden estate.

He visited Princeton frequently. There, he always was received with honor, esteem and respect, by both the town and the college. He had earned the A.B. degree at Princeton (Class of 1772) and the college had awarded him an LL.D. in 1803.

He lived comfortably but without ostentation. He always had at least one house servant. No national administration offered him any public position. His considerable income was spent on educating a number of protégés.

Not only were there protégés, there also was Luther Martin who had been the attorney general of Maryland when Colonel Burr had served as the attorney general of New York. He also had been one of the defense attorneys at the Burr trial in Richmond. Several years before Mr. Martin's death (he died on July 10, 1826), Colonel Burr took this physically ill and mentally befuddled old gentleman into his home and provided for all of his needs: food and drink, clothing, light and heat, spending money — as well as companionship.[2]

He seemed to develop a need for protégés — no doubt due to the double personal tragedy which was injected into his life, soon after his return to America.[3]

---

[2] See. Clarkson, Paul S. and R. Samuel Jett; *Luther Martin of Maryland*, Baltimore, Md., The Johns Hopkins Press, 1970.

[3] It should be noted, however, that Colonel Burr had a number of protégés before his period of four years in Europe. By his first marriage, he had two stepsons; Augustine James Frederick Prevost and John Bartow Prevost. He provided for the completion of their educational programs. For a number of years a member of the Burr household was Mlle. Nathalie deDelage deVolade who became Colonel Burr's ward and a "sister" to Theodosia during the French Revolution. Perhaps his best known protégé was John Vanderlyn, the painter who was educated in the United States and in Paris at Colonel Burr's expense.

Colonel Burr's only grandson, Aaron Burr Alston, died of a fever on May 29, 1812 at the age of ten years. This sad news reached him in New York about June 20. And the boy's mother, Colonel Burr's beloved daughter, Theodosia Burr Alston, wife of the governor of South Carolina, was lost at sea, while en route to visit her father. It is assumed that she died on January 1, 1813. Because of these two personal misfortunes, Colonel Burr said: "Now I am severed from the human race!" He no longer had any close relatives.

He did remarry, however, in 1833. The second Mrs. Burr was Mme. Eliza Bowen Jumel, the widow of M. Stephen Jumel.[4]

After a few months of happiness for both of them, in the magnificent and beautifully furnished big house on Harlem Heights, troubles developed and she brought suit for divorce. The case was heard in private, but the divorce was granted.[5]

_____

4 Ray Brown, in his biography of Mme. Jumel, called her: "America's most Beautiful, Fascinating, and Glamorous Woman." She was fifty-six years old at the time of her marriage to Colonel Burr and perhaps some of her beauty had faded but by that time, she had become America's most wealthy woman.

5 The charge against Colonel Burr, in the suit for divorce, was adultery. This had to be the case, because it was the only legal grounds for divorce in the state of New York at that time. Both then and now, evidence to prove adultery can be manufactured rather easily.

This raises the whole question of sex in Colonel Burr's life. On this subject, the writers of history seem to have used one approach when dealing with Burr and another one when dealing with his contemporaries. In the case of Colonel Burr, the approach has been one of overemphasis — in the cases of others, it has been one of overprotection.

It has been assumed that Colonel Burr had numerous amours and that he sired several illegitimate children. But practically nothing has been said about Mr. Jefferson's affairs de boudoir and his illegitimate children. (They were reputed to be octoroons born to his slave, Sally Hemings, who also was his wife's half-sister.) Perhaps the whole story of miscegenation at Monticello has not yet been fully told. Hamilton did make a public statement about his sordid affair with Mrs. Reynolds, when her husband went too far with his blackmail procedures. And Mrs. Hamilton may have had good reason to be jealous because a member of her im-

The decree was to have become effective on September 14, 1836. However, Colonel Burr died on the morning of that date. Thereafter, Madame Burr let it be known that she was the *widow* of the former vice-president of the United States.

During his final illness, Colonel Burr had competent, friendly care and attention. He then lived in a suitable apartment at Winant's Inn, Port Richmond, Staten Island, with windows facing New York harbor.

He was buried at Princeton, New Jersey on September 16, 1836, with full academic and military honors. The entire Princeton community — the college and the town — was involved in paying tribute to him. In due time a simple stone was erected to mark his grave, near those of his father and his grandfather.

---

mediate family was too attentive to "le petit fripon." Franklin was an acknowledged "playboy" and one of his illegitimate sons became the governor of New Jersey. Etc., etc., etc.

There has been a more or less tacit acknowledgment that one of Colonel Burr's protégés, Aaron Columbus Burr, was his "natural" son, born in France. This person was a good-looking, polite, well educated man who was a silversmith and goldsmith — a creative jeweler. He married and had one son, Aaron Hippolite Burr, who was a portrait painter. Aaron Hippolite Burr did not marry. He was the last possible direct descendant of Col. Aaron Burr. (died 1899).

All three of these men (Col. Aaron Burr, Aaron Columbus Burr and Aaron Hippolite Burr) had the dark hazel eyes which are inherited characteristics of various members of the Burr family.

Part V: Some Famous American Duels

IN THE BRITISH AMERICAN colonies along the Atlantic coast, from 1607 (Jamestown) until 1776 (The Declaration of Independence) and in the United States since 1776 (when it became an independent nation), hundreds of duels have been fought. Some of these duels have involved persons of considerable position and prominence. Political leaders, members of the learned professions, military and naval officers, social and civic leaders — these and many others have considered the "Code Duello" to be the proper means for settling various disputes.

Given this indisputable fact, it seems rather peculiar that historians have singled out only one of these many encounters for particular and persistent attention: namely, the Burr-Hamilton duel. In many of the books on American history, this is the only duel which is mentioned. Students are given the impression that it is the only American duel which has been historically important. It is the only duel on which a number of books have been written and published, even though some of the others deserve just as much attention.

It may be reasonable to conclude that the Burr-Hamilton duel has received all of this attention because it has been possible to use it as a means of vilifying Colonel Burr and as a means of making General Hamilton appear as some sort of a martyr. This appears to be the case, even though the writers of "history" have been required to depart somewhat from the plain truth and from the established facts in order to accomplish their purposes.

For the record, it may be noted that among the duels which have been fought in America are the following:

Mary Read (dressed as a man) vs. "Calico Jack" Rackham. On an island off the coast of Florida, circa 1718. Her second was Anne Bonny. The weapons were pistols, at ten paces. At the first fire, Rackham was wounded in the throat. Mary Read then ran toward him and slashed his neck with a cutlass. He survived both wounds. Soon after this duel, Mary Read died of a fever and Rackham was hanged as a pirate.

Henry Phillips vs. Benjamin Woodbridge. Near the Powder House on Boston Common, Boston, Massachusetts, July 3, 1728. (The weapons were swords.) Both were young men, engaged in business in Boston. Woodbridge was a graduate of Harvard College and a partner of Jonathan Sewall. Woodbridge was killed.

Gen. Lachlan McIntosh vs. the Hon. Button Gwinnett. In Georgia, just over the city line of Savannah, in

42

Chatham County, May 16, 1777. Gwinnett was a signer of the Declaration of Independence, a member of the Continental Congress and served as acting governor of Georgia. McIntosh was a general of the Georgia Militia and later was elected to Congress. Both men were wounded on the first exchange of fire. Gwinnett died three days later (May 19, 1777) at his home on St. Catherine's Island, Georgia. The wound received by McIntosh was not a serious one. Because Gwinnett died so soon after the Declaration of Independence was signed, his signature is rare and those which are known command a high price.

Gen. Horatio Gates vs. John Carter.
At Roxbury, Massachusetts, December 31, 1778.
Gates was a general in the Patriot army (the army of the American Revolution). Carter was a personal friend and a strong supporter of John Hancock. Neither participant was wounded.

Gen. James Jackson vs. George Wells.
In Georgia, near Savannah, in March 1780.
Jackson was the governor of the state of Georgia and Wells was the lieutenant governor. Wells was killed and Jackson was wounded. At some time later, General Jackson fought another duel, also near Savannah, with a prominent lawyer, Thomas Gibbons. This encounter took place in 1792.

George I. Eaker vs. Philip Schuyler Hamilton.
On a ledge of rock at Weehawken, New Jersey, November 24, 1801. Eaker was a lawyer and a Republican. Hamilton was the oldest son of Gen. Alexander Hamilton, one of the leaders of the Federalist party. Hamilton

43

was mortally wounded at the first fire and died on the following day. Eaker continued in his practice of law in New York City.

William H. Crawford vs. Peter Lawrence Van Alen.
At Fort Charlotte, near Mt. Carmel, South Carolina, 1803.
Crawford served in the United States Senate, as U.S. minister to France and as secretary of the treasury. He was one of the four candidates for president in the election of 1824. Van Alen was a prominent lawyer in Georgia (he had moved there from New York). Van Alen was mortally wounded. Crawford participated in at least one other duel — perhaps more than one. The one which is matter of record was with Gen. John Clark, on December 16, 1806, also at Fort Charlotte. Crawford was wounded in his left arm, at the first fire.

DeWitt Clinton vs. Col. John Swartwout.
At Weehawken, New Jersey, July 31, 1803.
Clinton was the nephew of Gov. George Clinton of New York, who became vice-president of the United States in 1805. He served as a U.S. senator, mayor of New York City and as the governor of New York. He was a Federalist. Swartwout was a Republican and a staunch supporter of Col. Aaron Burr. There were five exchanges of fire. Swartwout was wounded in the leg, at the fourth exchange and again at the fifth exchange of fire.

Col. Aaron Burr vs. Gen. Alexander Hamilton.
On a ledge of rock at Weehawken, New Jersey, July 11, 1804.
Colonel Burr had been a U.S. senator and was serving as vice-president of the United States. General Hamilton

44

had served as the first secretary of the treasury. Hamilton was mortally wounded at the first fire and he died on the following day. About one week previously, Colonel Burr had engaged in another duel, with John B. Church, Hamilton's brother-in-law. In that, neither Burr nor Church was wounded.

Frederick C. DeKraft vs. William R. Nicholson.
Near Syracuse, Sicily, on September 18, 1804.
Both men were midshipmen assigned to duty on the U.S. brig *Siren*. Nicholson was killed. DeKraft remained in the U.S. Navy and rose to the rank of rear admiral.

Gen. Andrew Jackson vs. Charles Dickinson.
At Harrison's Mill on Red River, Logan County, Kentucky, May 29, 1806. Jackson held a number of public offices and was elected president of the United States in 1828. He was the hero of the Battle of New Orleans (the battle that was fought after the war had ended), at the close of the War of 1812. Dickson was a prominent member of his community and the son-in-law of Capt. Joseph Erwin. Jackson was wounded and Dickinson was killed. General Jackson participated in at least a dozen other duels, over a period of about forty years.

William C. C. Claiborne vs. Daniel Clark.
At New Orleans, in the summer of 1807. Claiborne was serving as the governor of the territory of Orleans. Clark was a wealthy merchant of New Orleans and served as territorial delegate to the U.S. Congress. Neither man was wounded.

Lt. William E. Finch vs. Lt. Francis B. White.
On Border Street, East Boston, Massachusetts, September 25, 1808. Finch held a navy commission, White was commissioned in the U.S. Marine Corps. Both were assigned to duty on the frigate *Independence.* White was killed. Finch rose to the rank of commodore and commanded the U.S. fleet in the Mediterranean.

Col. John M. McCarty vs. Sen. Armistead T. Mason of Virginia.
At Bladensburg, Maryland, near Washington, D.C., on February 6, 1819. The two men were cousins but disagreed on political matters. The weapons were shotguns — at four paces! Mason fell dead at the first fire and McCarty was seriously wounded.

Commo. James Barron vs. Commo. Stephen Decatur.
Near Bladensburg, Maryland, just over the boundary of the District of Columbia, March 22, 1820. Both men were officers in the U.S. Navy and Decatur was a national hero due to his part in the undeclared war with Tripoli. Both men were wounded but Decatur received a mortal wound. Barron remained in the navy and became its senior commodore. Decatur's brother-in-law, Capt. James McKnight, husband of Ann Pine Decatur, also was killed in a duel (with Lt. Lawson), on October 14, 1802.

Thomas Hart Benton vs. Charles Lucas.
At Bloody Island, St. Louis, Missouri, August 11, 1817. And again on September 26, 1817. Both men were prominent lawyers. Benton was elected to the U.S. Senate from Missouri in 1820 and continued to serve as a senator for thirty years (five terms). He was the

father-in-law of Gen. John C. Fremont. In the first encounter Lucas was wounded and was unable to continue the fight. In the second encounter, he was killed. Benton participated in some five or six duels.

Commo. Oliver Hazard Perry vs. Capt. John Heath.
At Hoboken, New Jersey, across the Hudson River from New York City, in October, 1818. Perry's seconds were Commo. Stephen Decatur and Maj. James Hamilton. Heath's second was Lieutenant Desha. Perry was the hero of the Battle of Lake Erie (Put-in-Bay). Heath was the commandant of the detachment of U.S. Marines on the frigate *Java*. Perry had struck Heath for some infraction of the regulations. For this, Perry was court-martialed and Heath challenged him. The weapons were pistols at ten paces. The men were placed back to back. At a given signal, each was to step forward five paces, wheel about and fire at will. Both men followed the directions of their seconds. Heath fired at Perry but missed. Instead of firing, Perry handed his pistol to Decatur who then read a previously prepared statement. Upon hearing the statement, Heath indicated that he was satisfied and the encounter ended.

Gen. Sam Houston vs. Gen. William A. White.
On the farm of Sanford Duncan, in Kentucky, just across the state line from Tennessee, September 22, 1826. Houston had a remarkable political career: governor of Tennessee, president of the Republic of Texas, governor of the state of Texas. White was a prominent citizen of Nashville, Tennessee and a veteran of the Battle of New Orleans. Their argument arose from the political developments in Tennessee.

White received a serious wound in his hip, which confined him to his bed for a period of four months.

Henry Clay vs. John Randolph of Roanoke.
Near Little Falls (the shore of the Potomac, above Washington, D.C.), Virginia, April 8, 1826. Clay was a powerful political figure, member of the U.S. Senate, speaker of the House of Representatives and candidate for president. He was secretary of state in the cabinet of Pres. John Quincy Adams. John Randolph also was a powerful figure in national politics and was a U.S. senator from Virginia. Neither man was wounded but a ball from Clay's pistol passed through Randolph's coat. Henry Clay had fought a previous duel, on January 19, 1809, with Humphrey Marshall, in Indiana, across the Ohio River from Louisville, Kentucky. Marshall was a rabid Federalist politician, U.S. senator from Kentucky. Both men were slightly wounded and Clay was confined to his bedroom for three weeks. John Randolph had received a challenge from Gen. James Wilkinson, in 1807. Randolph refused to meet the challenger. Wilkinson then "posted" Randolph, at various places in Washington, as a "scoundrel, poltroon and coward." Randolph merely ignored the insult.

Gen. Felix Huston vs. Gen. Albert Sidney Johnston.
On the east side of the Lavaca River, outside Camp Independence, near Victoria, Texas, February 5, 1837. Huston was in command of Texas troops in an area southeast of San Antonio. Pres. Sam Houston sent Johnston to replace him. The two generals quarreled over the change in command and Huston challenged. The weapons were pistols, at twenty-five paces. Johnston was wounded on the sixth exchange of fire. He

recovered and the two men agreed to serve together, with Johnston in command. Johnston served as secretary of war for the Republic of Texas from 1838 to 1840. He served in the war with Mexico. He became a general in the Confederate army and was killed at the Battle of Shiloh in 1862.

William J. Graves vs. Jonathan Cilley.
Near Marlboro, Maryland (across the line from the District of Columbia). February 24, 1838. (The weapons were rifles!) Both of these antagonists were members of the House of Representatives, Graves from Kentucky and Cilley from Maine. Both were relatively young and politically ambitious. Cilley was killed at the third exchange of fire. At least half a dozen other congressmen were present and witnessed this duel.

Thomas F. Marshall vs. James W. Webb.
At Naaman's Creek (north of Wilmington), Delaware, June 27, 1842. Marshall was a member of Congress from Kentucky. Colonel Webb was the editor of the New York *Courier and Enquirer*. Colonel Webb was wounded in the leg on the second exchange of fire.

Thomas L. Clingman vs. William L. Yancey.
At Beltsville, Maryland (just over the line from the District of Columbia), January 13, 1845. Clingman was a member of Congress from North Carolina and Yancy was a member of Congress from Alabama. Police arrived and broke up the duel after one shot had been fired by each principal. Neither man was wounded.

Edward Heyward vs. August Belmont.
At Elkton, Maryland, September 27, 1841.

Belmont was a well-known financier and sportsman who married a niece of Oliver Hazard Perry. Heyward was the son of William Heyward, a prominent citizen of New York City. Belmont received a bullet in the right thigh.

Capt. Harry Maury vs. Baron Henry Arnous deRiviere.
In Mississippi, across the Alabama state line, near Mobile, in 1858. The weapons were Colt revolvers, at a distance of twelve paces. This duel resulted from rivalry between the two principals for the love of a Mobile belle, Miss Emily Blount. On the first fire, the Baron was struck in the chest but a gold coin in his vest pocket deflected the bullet and he was not injured. On the second exchange, the Baron was struck in the mouth. He was taken to the Blount mansion, where a surgeon removed the bullet. In due time, the Baron recovered. He and Emily were married in Paris, France, on July 4, 1865.

Judge George Pendleton Johnston vs. William Ferguson.
On Angel Island in San Francisco Bay, on August 21, 1858. Judge Johnston was the author of the anti-dueling law which recently had been passed by the California legislature! The weapons were pistols, the distance to start at ten paces but to be shortened with each ineffective exchange of fire. There were three ineffective exchanges, so that the distance was reduced to only six feet for the fourth exchange. This time, both men were hit. Johnston received a superficial flesh wound in his wrist. Ferguson received a bullet that shattered his right hip and severed an artery. He died three weeks later.

David S. Terry vs. David C. Broderick.

At Merced Lake, California, September 13, 1859. Terry served as a justice on the supreme court of California. Broderick was a United States senator from California. Broderick received a mortal wound and died on September 16. Broderick had fought a previous duel, with Judge William Smith, in 1852.

James Gordon Bennett (Jr.) vs. Frederick May.

At Slaughter's Gap, on the Delaware-Maryland state line, January 7, 1877. Bennett was of the New York *Herald* and May was affianced to his sister. The cause of the duel was "unbecoming conduct" by Bennett at the May residence in New York on New Year's Day, 1877. The Reverend Dr. George H. Hepworth (who wrote a weekly editorial for the *Herald*) was present to insure "fair play." Each principal fired one shot and both missed their mark, but "honor" was considered to have been satisfied and the duel ended.

Part VI: Bibliography: (Some Selected References)

A. CONCERNING COL. AARON BURR

Burr, Aaron; *The Private Journal of Aaron Burr*, (2 Vol.), edited by William H. Samson for William K. Bixby, Rochester, New York, The Genessee Press, 1903.

Clarkson, Paul S. and R. Samuel Jett; *Luther Martin of Maryland*, Baltimore, Maryland, The Johns Hopkins Press, 1970.

Daniels, Jonathan; *Ordeal of Ambition: Jefferson, Hamilton, Burr*, Garden City, New York, Doubleday & Company, Inc., 1970.

Geissler, Suzanne B.; "Aaron Burr and American Culture," Syracuse, N.Y., Unpublished Thesis, Honors Office, Hall of Languages, Syracuse University, 1971.

Henige, David P.; "Colonel Aaron Burr and the Election of 1800," Toledo, Ohio, Unpublished Thesis in University of Toledo Library, 1967.

Levy, Leonard D.; *Jefferson and Civil Liberties, The Darker Side*, Cambridge, Mass., Harvard University Press, 1963.

McCaleb, Walter F.; *New Light on Aaron Burr*, Austin, Texas, The Texas Quarterly Studies, University of Texas, 1963.

Parmet, Herbert S. and Marie B. Hecht; *Aaron Burr: Portrait of an Ambitious Man*, New York, The Macmillan Co., 1967.

Reed, V. B. and J. D. Williams, (editors); *The Case of Aaron Burr*, Boston, Houghton Mifflin Co., 1960 (Paper Bound).

Schachner, Nathan; *Aaron Burr: A Biography*, (Paperback Edition), New York, A. S. Barnes & Co., 1961.

Wandell, Samuel H. and Meade Minnigerode; *Aaron Burr*, (2 Vol.), New York, G. P. Putnam's Sons, 1925.

B. CONCERNING GEN. ALEXANDER HAMILTON

Bowers, Claude G.; *Jefferson and Hamilton*, Boston, Houghton Mifflin Co., 1925.

Boyd, Julian P.; *Number 7: Alexander Hamilton's Secret Attempts to Control American Foreign Policy*, Princeton, N.J., Princeton University Press, 1964.

Cooke, Jacob E., (editor), *Alexander Hamilton (A Profile)*, New York, Hill & Wang, Inc., 1967.

Hamilton, Allan McLane; *The Intimate Life of Alexander Hamilton*, New York, Charles Scribner's Sons, 1910.

Hamilton, John C.; *The Life of Alexander Hamilton*, (2 Vol.) Vol. I, New York, Halsted & Vorhies, 1834; Vol. II, Philadelphia, Appleton, 1840.

Loth, David; *Alexander Hamilton: Portrait of a Prodigy*, New York, Carrick & Evans, Inc., 1939.

Lomask, Milton; *Odd Destiny: A Life of Alexander Hamilton*, New York, Farrar, Straus & Giroux, 1969.

Malone, Dumas; *Jefferson and His Time*, (4 Vol.), Boston, Little, Brown & Co., 1948-1970.

Mitchell, Broadus; *Alexander Hamilton*, (2 Vol.), New York, The Macmillan Co., 1957 & 1962.

Schachner, Nathan; *Alexander Hamilton*, (Paperback Edition), New York, A. S. Barnes & Co., 1961.

Walters, Raymond, Jr.; *Albert Gallatin*, New York, The Macmillan Co., 1957.

Warshow, Robert Irving; *Alexander Hamilton, First American Business Man*, New York, Greenberg, Publisher, Inc., 1931.

C. CONCERNING DUELS AND DUELING

Andrews, Robert Hardy; "Politics at Pistol Point," *Mankind*, The Magazine of Popular History, Vol. II, No. 11, pp. 32-44 Incl., 1970.

Atkinson, John A.; *Duelling Pistols*, Harrisburg, Pa., Stackpole Books, 1966.

Benjamin, Lewis S.; *Famous Duels and Assassinations*, London, Jarrolds, 1929.

Boorstin, Daniel J.; *The Americans: The National Experience*, New York, Random House, 1965. Chapter 26, "How Southern Gentlemen Became Honorbound."

"C.J.R."; "Curiosities of the Law," *Notre Dame Lawyer*, December, 1926, Vol. 2, Page 50, etc.

Cochran, Hamilton; *Noted American Duels and Hostile Encounters*, Philadelphia, Chilton Books, A Division of Chilton Co., 1963.

Colton, Walter; *Remarks on Dueling*, Boston, Leavitt; Crocker & Brewster, 1828. (There was a reprint in 1895)

Kane, Harnett T.; *Gentlemen, Swords and Pistols*, New York, William Morrow & Co., 1951.

Millingen John Gideon; *The History of Duelling*, Including narratives of the Most Remarkable Personal Encounters

54

that have taken place from the Earliest Period to the Present Time, London, R. Bentley, 1841 (2 Vol.).

Sabin, Lorenzo; *Notes on Duels and Dueling*, Boston, 1859.

Seitz, Don C.; *Famous American Duels*, New York, Thomas Y. Crowell Co., 1929.

Syrett, Harold C. and Jean C. Cooke, (editors); *Interview in Weehawken*, Middletown, Conn., Wesleyan University Press, 1960.

Terrell, Col. William H. H.; *History of Noted Duels*, (Name of publisher and date of publication missing from library records).

D. CONCERNING MRS. THEODOSIA BURR ALSTON

Colver, Anne; *Theodosia*, New York, Holt, Rinehart & Winston, 1941, 1962.

Pidgin, Charles Felton; *Theodosia*, Boston, C. M. Clark Pub. Co., 1907.

Seton, Anya; *My Theodosia*, New York, Houghton Mifflin Co., 1941.

Van Doren, Mark (editor), *Correspondence of Aaron Burr and His Daughter Theodosia*, New York, Covici-Friede, Inc., 1929.

White, Mary Virginia Saunders, *Fifteen Letters of Nathalie Sumter*, Columbia, South Carolina, 1942.

E. CONCERNING MME. ELIZA BOWEN JUMEL BURR

Brown, Ray; *Madam Jumel: America's Most Beautiful, Fascinating and Glamorous Woman*, Jamestown, Va., Magna Carta Press, 1965.

Burr, Samuel Engle, Jr., "Mrs. Aaron Burr's Passport of 1853," *Autograph Collectors' Journal*, Summer Issue, 1951, Vol III, No. 4, pp. 13-17.

Duncan, William Cary; *The Amazing Madame Jumel*, New York, Frederick A. Stokes Co., 1935.

About the Author

IN ADDITION to being an historian, Dr. Burr has served as an educator, psychologist, school administrator and as a director of institutes, on the university level.

He holds academic degrees from Rutgers University, the University of Wisconsin, Columbia University and the University of Cincinnati. He was granted the title of "Professor of Education, Emeritus," by The American University, in 1968.

At present, he is a Visiting Professor of History at Weatherford College, Weatherford, Texas.

His active military service began during World War I and was resumed in World War II. He now holds the rank of Lieutenant Colonel, AUS, (Ret) and Lieutenant Colonel, CAP. He also is a Kentucky Colonel and Colonel of the Tenth Legion. He holds military decorations awarded by the United States Army and by the governments of five other nations.

In 1946, with the aid of a few other interested persons,

56

he founded The Aaron Burr Association and he has served as President General of A.B.A. since that time.

In addition to his three previous books on Col. Aaron Burr, he is the author of *Small Town Merchant, An Introduction to College, Our Flag and Our Schools, etc.*

He is a collector of postage stamps, coins, insulators, rock crystals and early Americana.

Dr. Burr is a member of various civic, patriotic and professional groups, including: The Society of Colonial Wars, Sons of the American Revolution, The Order of Lafayette, The American Legion, Rotary International, and The Sovereign Order of St. John of Jerusalem (Knights Hospitalers).

He has traveled extensively in the United States and he has visited thirty foreign countries. During the spring and summer of 1964, he lectured at various colleges, universities and cultural centers in Germany, France and England.

Dr. Burr's primary interest in the field of American history is the life and career of Col. Aaron Burr and the life of his daughter, Mrs. Theodosia Burr Alston. His second area of interest is the life and career of Jefferson Davis, president of the Confederate States of America, and the life of his wife, Mrs Varina Howell Davis, who was a member of the New Jersey branch of the Burr family.